PALOMA BLANCA

Illustrated by PAULA KRANZ

WHAT IF I FEEL...

HAPPY

W. Books

Dados Internacionais de Catalogação na Publicação (CIP) de acordo com ISBD

B236w Barbieri, Paloma Blanca Alves

What if I feel... happy / Paloma Blanca Alves Barbieri ; traduzido por Karina Barbosa dos Santos ; ilustrado por Paula Kranz. – Jandira : W. Books, 2025.
32 p. ; 24cm x 24cm. – (What if I feel...)

Tradução de: E se eu sentir... felicidade
ISBN: 978-65-5294-225-8

1. Literatura Infantil. 2. Emoções. 3. Sentimentos. 4. Felicidade. 5. Psicologia. 6. Saúde. 7. Saúde mental. I. Santos, Karina Barbosa dos. II. Kranz, Paula. III. Título. IV. Série.

CDD 028.5
CDU 82-93

2025-1830

Elaborada por Vagner Rodolfo da Silva - CRB-8/9410

Índice para catálogo sistemático:
1. Literatura infantil 028.5
2. Literatura infantil 82-93

This book was printed in Melon Slices and Metallophile font.

This is a W. Books publication, a division of Grupo Ciranda Cultural.
© 2025 Ciranda Cultural Editora e Distribuidora Ltda.
Publisher: Elisângela da Silva
Text © Paloma Blanca A. Barbieri
Illustrations © Paula Kranz
Translation: Karina Barbosa dos Santos
Proofreading: Adriane Gozzo
Design: Fernando Nunes / Cover: Natalia Renzzo

First published in June 2025
www.cirandacultural.com.br

All rights reserved. No part of this publication may be reproduced, stored in a retrieval system, or transmitted in any form or by any means, electronic, mechanical, photocopying, recording, or otherwise, without written permission of the copyright holder, nor may it be circulated bound or covered in any manner other than that in which it was published, or without such conditions beholden to subsequent purchasers.

"Emotions are the colors of the soul; they are spectacular and incredible. When you don't feel, the world becomes dull and colorless."
William P. Young

I dedicate this book to my gigantic family (especially my mother, Creusa), who has given me and continues to give the most beautiful and diverse emotions!

From the beginning to the end of the day, I feel a whirlwind of emotions.

Out of all of them, my favorite is **happiness**!

When I'm happy, my heart feels warm all over.

I can't even hide this feeling because my eyes shine, and I can't stop smiling!

When my family or friends come play with me, I feel so happy that I can't stop giggling.

The funny thing is, in moments like these, time flies so fast that it feels like it's soaring!

When I make a new friend, my heart fills with joy too.

After all, it's so wonderful to have someone to share games...

... adventures, and, of course, lots of mischief with!

Some moments make me so happy that I always want to share them.

Like when a new family member arrives!

And also my birthday!

Surprise!

When someone tickles me, it feels like happiness is bursting out of my chest!

The same thing happens when I play tag, hide-and-seek, or ride my bike.

When I'm happy, I feel like singing, jumping, and dancing!

A feeling this good is even better when it's shared!

To me, happiness is the most amazing emotion of all.

It makes the person who feels it happy and spreads joy to everyone around them!

After all, happiness is contagious!

How do you feel today?

Thankful

Sad

Happy

Angry

Afraid

Loving

Take a little moment to talk about how you're feeling right now.

Talking About Happiness

Feeling happy is so wonderful that there's no downside to it! Let's take a moment to reflect on this feeling.

- What makes you happy?
- How do you feel when you're happy?
- When was the last time you felt happy?
- What did it feel like?

Did you know that happiness is a feeling you can attract? That's right! When we do what we love, spend time with the people we care about, and show kindness and generosity, we welcome the best emotions into our lives. Thinking happy thoughts and talking about good things are also great ways to bring more happiness into your days. How about saying these affirmations out loud to invite even more joy into your life? Let's do it!

- I am very happy!
- I am happy because I have a wonderful family!
- I am kind, I am good, I am happy!
- I am happy because I am deeply loved!

Children, Animals, and Feelings

Children are usually fascinated by pets, and it's no wonder why! Besides being loving and great friends, pets bring joy to a home, improve our health, and create a wonderful sense of well-being.

Having a pet (whether it's a kitten, a puppy, or a bunny) can teach children important values like patience, respect, kindness, affection, and responsibility.

Also, when they're with animals, children find the confidence and self-esteem they need to solve their problems and even deal with their own feelings.

A Message for the Family

The journey of discovering emotions can be both surprising and challenging for children, especially because they don't always know how to express what they're feeling. That's why this book aims to help little ones understand how and when the feeling of happiness appears and why it's so important to experience it in every moment.

In this process of emotional discovery, families and educators are invited to see happiness from a different perspective: the child's! After all, children have a unique and special way of perceiving everything happening around them.

Dealing with emotions isn't always easy, whether for adults or children. That's why the sooner little ones understand their feelings, the sooner they will develop autonomy and confidence, essential skills for navigating this incredible journey we all share: life!

PALOMA BLANCA was born in a coastal city in São Paulo. Passionate about languages, she pursued a degree in literature and specialized in translation and teaching.

She has loved writing since childhood; in her stories and poems, she would express everything she felt, as writing became the perfect way for her to explore and understand her emotions. Writing this book has been a true gift, one she hopes to share with families, especially with children who, just like she did in her childhood, wish to learn how to navigate the whirlwind of emotions that arise throughout life.

PAULA KRANZ is the mother of two wonderful girls. When she became a mother, her heart was flooded with countless emotions. She embraced the opportunity to transform all the fear, sadness, anger, and immense joy she experienced into feelings that helped her grow as a person.

Together with her daughters, she reconnected with the magical world of childhood. In recent years, alongside playing pretend, building sandcastles, and doodling, she has also specialized in children's books, illustrating many published works. She is filled with dreams and an eagerness to capture the delicacy and lightness of childhood, bringing to life the magic, the sparkle in children's eyes, and their unique way of seeing the world—something they share with us every single day.